KROEUNG

 គ្រឿង

Cambodian Cooking with Chef T

Visoth Tarak Ouk
Christine Su

Library of Congress Cataloging-in-Publication Data

Kroeung: Cambodian Cooking with Chef T / by Visoth Tarak Ouk and Christine Su

Cover photos courtesy of Maly Uch and Sokunthea Oum

Note: To maintain the flow of the text, full photo credits are included in a separate section at the end of the book, rather than in captions. All photos used with permission or license.

ISBN (paper) 979-8-218-08123-2

First edition

Dedication

For my sister, Chomvorttei "Chom" Ouk
(1984-2010)

Photo courtesy of the Ouk family

Your love for life and beautiful spirit inspired me
to pursue my dreams of becoming a chef.

I will hold you forever in my heart.

- Chef T

Acknowledgements

Writing this book has been a journey we (Chef T and Christine) have taken together. And, of course, there are so many others without whom the project would not have come to fruition. While it is not possible to list every individual here, or to detail all the ways in which they have supported us, there are many who have gone above and beyond to see us succeed, and we thank them here.

We apologize for any inadvertent omissions. We love you all!

ដោយសេចក្ដីគោរពដ៏ខ្ពង់ខ្ពស់បំផុត ខ្ញុំសូមអរគុណ។

Larry Ambrosi
Jhoanna Belfer
Eric Cardoso
Shawn Chan
L. Pheakdey Chea
Jenny Chea-Vaing
Krystal M. Chuon
Thuy Vo Dang
Julie Daniels
Rany Fischer
Mike Gin
DJ Hunny Hach
Ratha Hanh
Rithy Hanh
Terri Henry
Scott Hewitt
Chan Hopson
Mark Hopson
Kimhouy Hou
Phung Huynh
Sanghak Kan
Mary Kheng
Danielle Khim
Ratha Chuon Kim
Mea Lath

Clare Le Bras
Chanwatha San Limon
Chef Victor Lopez
praCh Ly
Sovanna Mao
Tey Plong Nelms
Christina Nhek
Chet and Sash Nin
Jeff Osbourne
Sokunthea Oum
Chef Anthony Overton
Chad Phuong
Chef Pierre
Sophin Zoe Pruong-McCreery
Darachan Ros
Shawn Piseth Ros
Chhany Sak-Humphry
John Sangmeister
Hak Seang
Caylee So
Charles Song
Sayon Syprasoeuth
Richard Thiounn
Maly Uch
Kalean Ung Breen

Ankara Uy Has
Olary Yim
Art Theatre of Long Beach
Asian World Film Festival
BelCanto Books
Cambodia Town Film Festival (CTFF)
Cambodia Town, Inc.
Cambodian Student Society @ Cal State Long Beach
Gladstone's Long Beach
Khmer Generations Project
Khmer Women's Alliance
Long Beach City College
Long Beach Food & Bev.
Long Beach Public Libraries
Mark Twain Neighborhood Library
Rajana Threads
SEARCH Ctr.
The Federal Bar
United Cambodian Community (UCC)
Visit Cambodia Town Long Beach

and of course, a million thanks to our loved ones, especially:

➤ Baky Sar and Phoenix Ouk, as well as the entire Ouk and Sar families; (Chef T)
➤ Don Fallon , Elizabeth Su, Peanut, and Miss Beans (RIP); (Christine)

SOUTHEAST
ASIA
MAP

MYANMAR

LAOS

Naypyidaw

Hanoi

Vientiane

THAILAND

VIETNAM

Bangkok

Manila

CAMBODIA

PHILIPPINES

Phnom Penh

BRUNEI

Banda Seri Begawan

MALAYSIA

Kuala Lumpur

SINGAPORE

Jakarta

INDONESIA

Dili

EAST TIMOR

Image: muchmania/Adobe Stock

SITE II   SITE B   Cambodia

KHAO-I-DANG

PHANAT NIKHOM
(CHONBURI)

SISOPHON

ANGKOR WAT

BATTAMBANG

SIEM REAP

PURSAT

KAMPONG
CHHNANG

PHNOM PENH

SIHANOUKVILLE

KAMPOT

Map ©2022 by C. Su/SEARCH

vi

About Cambodia

Cambodia is one of the eleven nations of Southeast Asia, along with Brunei, Indonesia, Laos, Malaysia, Myanmar, Philippines, Singapore, Thailand, Timor Leste, and Vietnam. Most of mainland Southeast Asia (now Thailand, Laos, and Vietnam) was at one time part of the vast Khmer Empire. From the 9th to the 14th centuries, the Khmer Empire was concentrated in Angkor in the northwest of modern-day Cambodia, where Khmer monarchs created massive and elaborate stone temples.[1]

During the 12th century, King Suryavarman II (r. 1113—1150 AD) built the magnificent temple known as Angkor Wat, dedicated to the Hindu god, Vishnu. The Khmer Empire reached its zenith in the 13th century under the rule of King Jayavarman VII (r. 1181-1218), who constructed the massive Bayon, part of Angkor Thom, as a shrine dedicated to the Buddha.

In the centuries following the Angkor period the Empire was repeatedly attacked, with the Thai and the Vietnamese competing for control. By the 19th century, the French had begun to colonize much of mainland Southeast Asia (which they called Indochina). In 1863, Cambodia became a French protectorate, and remained under French jurisdiction until 1953.

As background to the influx of Cambodian refugees to the U.S. which began in the late 1970s and 1980s, below is an abbreviated timeline of modern Cambodian history.[2]

1941: The French declare Norodom Sihanouk (b. 1922) King of Cambodia, then a French protectorate.

1953: Under His Majesty King Norodom Sihanouk, Cambodia declares its independence as a sovereign nation.

1954: As per the Geneva Accords, the French agree to withdraw from Cambodia, Laos, and Vietnam.

1955: King Norodom Sihanouk abdicates from the throne to pursue politics.

1960s: A group of young Cambodian scholars educated in France returns and begins to radicalize the Communist Party of Kampuchea (CPK). Norodom Sihanouk names his communist opponents *Khmer Krahom* (Red Khmer); or in French, the "Khmer Rouge."

1965: U.S. involvement in the Vietnam War escalates. Prince Sihanouk breaks off relations with the United States.

1969: U.S. President Richard Nixon begins secret bombing of Cambodia, killing or displacing tens of thousands of Cambodian villagers.

1975: Cambodia falls under the control of the radical communist Khmer Rouge (KR). The KR empty the cities and force the population into the countryside to undertake hard agricultural labor. Millions die from overwork, disease, starvation, torture, or execution during the regime.

1979: Vietnamese soldiers overthrow the Khmer Rouge, but war and unrest continue. Cambodians flee, mostly to the Thai border; many linger for years in refugee camps.

1980: The U.S. passes the Refugee Act, allowing Southeast Asian Refugees to resettle throughout the U.S. Between 1980 and 1985, more than 125,000 Cambodian refugees enter the U.S.

TABLE OF CONTENTS

TABLE OF CONTENTS (cont.)

Introduction

by Christine Su

I first met "Chef T" at a Khmer Student Coalition Conference hosted by Cal State Long Beach in 2016. As he often does for community events, Chef T was cooking and serving food at the conference, as well as managing a handful of assistants and volunteers. He was rushing around, taking care of last-minute changes and accommodating requests. Sweat had broken out on his forehead, and it was clear many things and people wanted his attention. Still, Chef T had spoken earlier as the keynote at the conference, and after hearing his story, I had to meet him. He likely doesn't remember this, but I stopped him as he was running by, introduced myself, and told him how much I enjoyed his speech. He stopped, thanked me, told me how honored he was to part of a Khmer-centered event, and then gave me a big hug. I told him that I would like to write about his experiences one day, and he said absolutely, we should make that happen. Little did I know that years later, I would have the privilege of recording and sharing some of Chef T's favorite recipes – and stories about his life – with you.

Writing about Cambodian food in the United States, some reviewers and critics make almost-immediate comparisons to Thai, Vietnamese, or Chinese food. But doing so does Cambodia and Khmer cooks an injustice, because while it reflects influences from its geographic neighbors, as well as other global tastes, Khmer cuisine is much more complex than a "kind of like [Thai/Vietnamese/Chinese] food" descriptor.

Khmer food and flavors stand on their own, even if less recognizable to Western-trained palates. Because of the relative lack of visibility of Cambodian cooking, especially in the U.S., some writers have as gone as far to say that Khmer cuisine needs to be "saved from extinction." This is not entirely accurate; if there are Cambodians, there will be Cambodian food.

What is more accurate is to say that following the Khmer Rouge regime (1975-1979), during which more than 2 million Cambodians perished, much of the knowledge about specific Cambodian recipes and cooking methods died as Cambodians with that knowledge themselves died. Furthermore, during the regime Cambodians were given very little food--oftentimes only tiny portions of watery rice porridge--and after the regime fell, food was still scarce. Focused on survival, people acquired what they could, with understandably less attention to culinary techniques or exact ingredients than to availability.

Consequently, in the aftermath of the war and genocide, recipes may have been recreated, modified, or adapted to different circumstances and environments.

When Cambodians came to the U.S. as refugees in the 1980s, few would have had the financial resources or business know-how (not to mention physical or emotional energy or English fluency) to open restaurants. Staples in Cambodian cooking like galangal, lemongrass, kaffir or makrut lime leaves, and palm sugar were not always readily available in their new cities or neighborhoods, and it would have been challenging to purchase the bulk amounts needed to cook for large numbers of customers. As a result, Khmer food did not cross over into U.S. eateries as quickly as other Asian cuisines.

Moreover, eating Khmer food is associated with family. Prior to the Khmer Rouge regime, family members ate together. Cambodians would often leave work and return home for lunch to eat shared plates with their families, even in the cities. One of the methods used by the Khmer Rouge to break down the family unit was forcing Cambodians to eat silently in communal dining halls with other workers, separated from family members. A return to eating food served at home represented a return to family, to normalcy and life before the Khmer Rouge.

In recent years there has been more interest in Cambodian food and cooking, especially by members of the 1.5 (those born in Cambodia or the refugee camps who came to the U.S. at a young age) and 2.0 (those born in the U.S.) generations of Cambodian Americans. They have begun to ask their elders about pre-war and regional cuisine; they have written down recipes theretofore passed down only through oral tradition or hands-on experience; and they have begun cooking Khmer food themselves. They are dedicated to honoring and sustaining Khmer cuisine, but also open to incorporating elements of their own cooking and eating experiences. One of these individuals is Visoth Tarak Ouk, "Chef T."

Writing this book with Chef T has been an honor, and I am so grateful to Chef and his family for sharing their anecdotes, whether humorous, sorrowful, astonishing, or poignant (or somehow all of these at the same time) with me, and for trusting me to relate their stories to a wider audience. This book provides just a "taste" of the dozens of delicious Khmer dishes—sour, savory, sweet—Khmer food is truly unique. I hope that as you read the book and try out the recipes, that you can hear Chef's voice and feel his passion for his art.

A Note from Chef T

by Visoth Tarak Ouk

If anyone had told me when I was in my twenties that I would one day be a college graduate, an executive chef at a well-respected, busy restaurant, or a father with a beautiful wife and son, I would have thought you were crazy. My life hasn't always been joyful; in fact, for some years you could actually say it was dismal.

As the son of two survivors of the genocidal Khmer Rouge regime in Cambodia, I inherited a lot of the trauma and pain they endured. Cambodian refugees in the U.S. lived erratic lives in situations and environments that were confusing, frightening, unstable. Without even knowing they were doing so, many passed this trauma on to their children. I was one of those who lost themselves in the chaos of living in an under-resourced area, learning a new language, going to a new school, and trying to adapt to an unfamiliar culture. I longed to feel safe, supported, and encouraged at home, but my parents struggled to put food on the table, working long hours to do so, and were exhausted and grief-stricken themselves. Like many in my generation, especially young men, I felt isolated, and consequently looked for support and guidance elsewhere. I fell into gang and street life. Unfortunately, doing so led me down a disastrous road and I found myself engaging in regrettable behaviors. Violence surrounded me. My future looked bleak.

Then in 2010, I lost one of my sisters in a tragic car accident. Her death shocked me. She was very smart and hardworking, kind of like a "golden child," just weeks away from receiving a master's degree from Cal State Fullerton. She was only 25 years old. While she and I were very different, we were closely bonded. This was definitely a pivotal moment for me. After she died, I began to think about the fragility of life, how someone's life can be over in the blink of an eye. I asked myself what my purpose was in this life, and I saw that if I was honest with myself, I was pretty aimless, and that had to change. So I turned to the one thing I had always loved, cooking.

I had started training in the culinary arts program at Long Beach City College in 2002 but gave up after a while. After my sister died, however, I reenrolled and began again with renewed purpose and energy. Sometimes it took me 3 hours to walk from my house to school. At first, I didn't have money for books, so I asked my classmates to photocopy chapters from their books so I could do the assignments. I would study long into the night, when many times I would have rather slept; but I had a vision: I was going to succeed as a chef.

Here in this book I present to you just a few of my favorite recipes. In the future, I will publish a full-on cookbook (which I hope you will look out for) but for this first effort, I simply wanted to write about some of the dishes, and the individuals from whom I learned to make them, that continue to inspire me. Thank you for your support and love. Please enjoy.

A variety of Cambodian foods and condiments. Photo: Mary Kheng

Chapter 1: Cambodian Flavors

Cambodian food is extraordinary, a veritable celebration of different flavors and tastes. Contrary to what those new to it may believe, most Khmer cuisine is not hot. Chilies are usually added to basic recipes according to the individual chef's (or customer's) taste, but they are not required. Below are some of the flavor profiles that epitomize Khmer cuisine.

Kroeung ingredients. Photo: Sokunthea Oum

Kroeung

What is ក្រឿង (*kroeung*)? An essential ingredient in much of Khmer cooking, *kroeung* is an herb and spice paste made from lemongrass, turmeric, galangal or ginger, garlic, kaffir lime leaves, shallots, and salt. The ingredients are ground together using a mortar and pestle, which releases the wonderful and aromatic oils and flavors of each ingredient.

The yellow *kroeung* paste that results is used as the base for many Cambodian dishes, including *somlor machu kroeung* and *amok*. *Kroeung* can be purchased ready-made, but there is nothing like the taste of freshly-pounded *kroeung*.

Basic Yellow *Kroeung* Recipe

Ask three people how to make *kroeung* and you may receive three different responses, because each individual will adjust the recipe according to his or her tastes. But there are five ingredients that are always in traditional *kroeung*: lemongrass, turmeric, galangal, garlic, and kaffir/makrut lime leaves. Below is a basic recipe for *kroeung*.

INGREDIENTS

Ingredient (English)	ឈ្មោះ (ភាសាខ្មែរ)	Amount
lemongrass	ស្លឹកក្រៃ	2 or 3 stalks (1 cup chopped)
turmeric	រមៀត	½ tsp fresh chopped or powdered
galangal*	រំដេង	1 root (2 tbsp peeled, chopped)
garlic	ទឹមស	1 whole garlic bulb, peeled
Kaffir/Makrut lime leaves	ស្លឹកក្រូច	6 large, center veins removed

Cooking directions:

1. Chop the lemongrass (bottom third of stalks only) and place into the mortar, and pound with pestle until lemongrass is mashed.
2. Add each of the other ingredients: galangal, lime leaves, garlic, and turmeric into the paste, making sure all ingredients are incorporated well.

Some cooks prefer lime zest over lime leaves, and some may add salt, shallots, and/or fish sauce to the basic ingredients based upon individual preferences.

*If galangal is unavailable, you may use ginger, although the taste will differ slightly.

Note: Adding dried peppers or chilies changes the basic paste to *kroeung krahom* (red *kroeung*), used in dishes such as *somlor kari*.

Prahok

What is ប្រហុក (*prahok*)? *Prahok* is a salted, fermented fish paste that is used to season many Khmer dishes. Both its smell and its flavor are potent and distinctive.

Traditionally made from a local mud carp called *trey riel*, *prahok* is used in soups, sauces, or dips. Unique dishes include *prahok ktis* (minced pork fried with *kroeung*, *prahok*, coconut milk, and spices), and *prahok ang* (*prahok* wrapped in banana leaves and cooked over a fire). To truly experience Khmer food, you must try it!

Prahok. Photo: Pakse/Wikipedia

Trey riel

Skar thnout

What is ស្ករត្នោត (*skar thnout*)? The Khmer have been producing *skar thnout*, or palm sugar, from the sap of palm sugar trees (palmyra palms) for centuries.

During the dry season, the sap of the tree's flowers is collected and boiled until it reduces, then set out to dry and crystalize. The result is a light brown sugar with notes of caramel and a wonderful floral aroma.

Skar thnout. Photo: Sovanna Mao

Fresh tamarind. Photo: YarikL/Adobe Stock

Ampil

What is អំពិល (*ampil*)? Ampil, known in English as tamarind, is a sweet and/or sour fruit that grows in pods. When cracked, inside the pods you will find seeds covered in a thick, sticky pulp. The tangy pulp or juice is used in sauces and soups and dried tamarind powder is added to dishes as a seasoning, but if you come across ripe tamarind, you can also eat it right out of the pod. ឆ្ងាញ់ណាស់ (Delicious)!

Mric Kampot

What is ម្រេចកំពត (*mric Kampot*)? Kampot province (highlighted in red on the map at right) has the ideal conditions (a humid climate and quartz-rich soil) for growing *mric*, or pepper, and Kampot peppercorns are highly prized. Kampot pepper can be used in its fresh, green state, or in one of its dried forms: black, red, or white. Use Kampot pepper whenever a recipe calls for pepper--you will taste the delicious difference.

Image: NordNordWest/Wikimedia

Black, red, and white peppercorns.
Photo: TravelPhotography/Adobe Stock

Chapter 2: Sour ជូរ

What is *Somlor Machu*?

Growing up, *somlor machu* was my favorite soup. It is a staple of Cambodian cuisine, and my mom and grandma often made this when my siblings and I needed comfort, or when the whole family would gather to eat. This *somlor*, which in its simplest form is a salty, sour, herb-forward broth, to which protein and vegetables are added, represented unity, love, and togetherness. It is a classic Khmer dish.

I watched my mom lean over the stove, making a big pot of *somlor machu* for everyone – quite an endeavor with the number of family members we had (I'm one of nine children!). Its ingredients include the delicious vegetable known to Khmer as *trakuon* (morning glory or water spinach in English) grown throughout the Cambodian countryside, and *prahok*, our salty, fermented fish paste that is an essential element of Khmer cuisine. The ជូរ *machu* (sour) taste comes from the tamarind. And of course, it has *kroeung*, which imparts its distinctive lemony flavor (there's really no way to adequately describe the taste of *kroeung* – you just have to try it!).

As the years went by, I too made many pots of *somlor machu*, and as I am inclined to do, I experimented with putting my own flare on this traditional dish. Specifically, for example, for *somlor machu kroeung sach koh* (Cambodian sour soup with beef), I added jalapenos and Thai chilies, because I like some heat. Generally speaking, Khmer food is not overly hot or spicy, but I like to make things my own. Another variation on *somlor machu* is *somlor machu youn / somlor machu peng poh* (Cambodian sour soup with tomatoes), with a lighter broth. In my version, I added more color, more texture, more tang to the basic recipe.

I hope you feel the warmth of family and togetherness as you eat and enjoy your versions of this dish.

-Chef T

Somlor Machu Kroeung Sach Koh
(Cambodian Sour Soup with Beef)

This dish is a household favorite. To me its rich broth and earthy flavor reflects the soul of hardworking farming families and represents "home."

As mentioned, we ate *somlor machu* regularly while I was growing up. Yet this particular version, *somlor machu kroeung sach koh*, was something my father made rather than my mother or grandmother. My father didn't cook much, but this was one of the things he loved making – and we approved!

So when I make this, I think of my father and hope I am making him proud. This dish lives in my heart.

Me with my father in front of our home in Oakland, California, 1980s.

Photo courtesy of Chef T.

Chef's note: one of the great things about *somlor machu kroeung sach koh* is its versatility. You can customize it beyond the basic ingredients based upon your taste preferences. Some make it with a lot of *trakuon*, and some add their favorite vegetables. Some use less water, to make it more like a stew, while some add more water, to make it more soup-like. I add a bunch of chilies because I like it spicy!

Chef T's *Somlor Machu Kroeung Sach Koh*

Cooking Time
1 hr

Serves 4-6

INGREDIENTS

1 cup *kroeung*

1 pound beef (any cut), sliced

1 pound beef tripe & lungs

4 tbsp cooking oil (e.g., canola)

2 cups beef stock

water (add to make the desired amount of soup)

1 cup tamarind paste or ½ cup tamarind powder

1 pound *trakuon* (morning glory/water spinach)

5 dwarf Chinese eggplants, halved

4 stalks celery, diced

3 tbsp fish sauce

2 tbsp *prahok*

2 tbsp *skar thnout* (may substitute cane sugar if palm sugar is not available)

4 jalapeño peppers (optional)

3 red Thai chilies (optional)

Cooking directions:

1. Combine sliced beef with the *kroeung*, and sauté in a deep pan for 5-10 minutes.

2. Add tripe & lungs.

3. Pour in beef stock and water, then add the tamarind.

4. Bring to a boil and then simmer on low for 15 minutes.

5. Add in the *trakuon*, celery, eggplants, and jalapeños (optional).

6. Add the fish sauce and/or salt to taste.

7. Add the *prahok*.

8. Stir in the *skar thnout* or sugar.

9. Simmer until all meats are thoroughly cooked.

10. If you like it spicy, add Thai chilies.

Serve with white rice. Enjoy!

11

Somlor machu kroeung sach koh. Photo: Maly Uch

In addition to *kroeung*, *somlor machu kroeung sach koh* also highlights *trakuon*, known in English as morning glory or water spinach, a vegetable which grows in abundance in Cambodia. It is inexpensive but delicious, used often in soups or stir-fries.

Above: *trakuon* Photo: Christine Su
Right: fresh, uncooked *trakuon*. Photo: Maly Uch

Somlor Machu Yuon / Somlor Machu Peng Poh
(Cambodian sour soup with fish and tomatoes)

This is another of my favorite soups. (It's difficult to pick just one!) My mom would make it for us kids when we were feeling down or sad and needed comfort, as it is very soothing. The *somlor*'s sweet and sour flavors come from the *ampil* (tamarind), *peng poh* (tomatoes), and *plae manoa* (pineapple). It is usually made with fish. I like to add other types of seafood as well.

Somlor machu yuon 'royale'. Photo: Chef T

I call my version *somlor machu yuon "royale"* because I use high-end seafood proteins in it – although these were out of the reach of our family (and most Cambodian refugee families) growing up. But I love experimenting with traditional recipes. Here I transformed what started off as a "peasant" dish into a delicious creation fit for royalty.

-Chef T

INGREDIENTS

- 1-2 tbsp tamarind pulp
- 1 cup hot water
- 5 garlic cloves, minced
- 2 oz fish filets (preferably catfish)
- 2 cups pineapple chunks (canned/fresh)
- 4 tomatoes, cut into qtrs
- 10 lotus roots
- 2 tbsp fish sauce
- 1 tsp soy sauce
- ½ teaspoon white or black Kampot pepper
- ½ lb shrimp
- 1 whole Maine lobster, cut into sections
- 3 river prawns (whole: membrane will form a red swirl in the broth)
- ½ cup tarragon, chopped
- 1 tsp lemongrass, finely chopped
- 1 cup Thai basil, chopped
- 1 galangal root
- 4 Thai chilies or jalapeño peppers (optional)

Chef T's
Somlor Machu Youn "Royale"

Cook time
1 hr

Serves 4-6

Cooking Directions:

1. Strain the tamarind pulp through a mesh strainer, adding the hot water to soften it. Discard large pieces of tamarind, but keep the strained liquid and put it aside.

2. In a medium-hot pan, fry half of the garlic until it becomes golden brown and aromatic.

3. Add the catfish filets, taking care to get a nice sear on them. Put them aside.

4. In a medium pot add the rest of the fresh garlic, pineapple, lotus roots, and tomatoes. Stir lightly with a spatula until all ingredients are mixed.

5. Add in fish sauce, soy sauce, white pepper and tamarind liquid to the mixture. Cover mixture with water and bring the soup to a boil.

6. Once the soup is boiling, add the proteins: fish filet, prawns, shrimp, and lobster. Add the tarragon, lemongrass, half of the basil, and galangal. Simmer for 15-20 minutes, gently stirring every now and then.

7. Ladle the *somlar* into bowls, and add more fried garlic, additional Thai basil, and Thai chilies or jalapeños to taste.

8. Serve with white rice.

Chapter 3: Savory សេជាតិ

Fish comprises more than 60 percent of Cambodians' protein intake, and is the second most consumed food, after rice. Freshwater fish are harvested from one of the many waterways that traverse Cambodia, including the Mekong River, the Tonle Sap River, and the Tonle Sap Lake, and many dishes highlight fish, such as the decadent and delicious *amok*.

Amok

The term "*amok*" is a verb that describes the method of cooking by steaming food in a banana leaf.

This delicious creation, usually made with fish (snakehead or catfish), is not an everyday dish, as it takes a long time to prepare. Rather, it is reserved for special occasions: dinners with special guests, Buddhist holy days, or celebrations such the annual Water Festival (*Bon Om Touk*). Some Cambodians believe *amok* originated centuries ago and was prepared for royalty.

My version of *amok* uses king salmon rather than whitefish, and thus I call it "*Amok* King." It has all the textures and flavors of an original *amok*, but I have elevated it slightly with the choice of higher-end protein. This also speaks to the mythos about its regal roots.

Individual *amok* in banana leaf.
Photo: Maly Uch

Amok King
Photo: Chef T

Amok "King"

INGREDIENTS

2 roots of galangal
1 root of ginger
6 cloves garlic
3 kafir lime leaves
½ cup peanuts
3 tbsp turmeric
½ cup kroeung
Banana leaves

2 pounds King Salmon
3 stems Swiss chard or kale, chopped
16 oz coconut milk

3 duck eggs
green onions (chopped)
chilies
Salmon roe (eggs)

Cook time: approx. 1 hr prep time; additional 10 minutes to steam the *amok*

Serves 4-6 (individual servings in banana leaf)

Cooking Directions:

1. Peel the galangal, ginger, and garlic and chop coarsely.

2. Put kafir lime leaves, peanuts, and turmeric into a food processor, and add the *kroeung*. Blend until smooth.

3. Cut up king salmon into equally sized cubes. Heat oil in a pan and add the salmon, being careful not to overcook it.

4. Add the blended *kroeung* mixture to the salmon and sautee without breaking down the fish.

5. Add kale or Swiss chard and stir.

6. Add 12 oz of the coconut milk; simmer 15-20 minutes until kale or chard softens.

7. In a bowl, mix the duck eggs with the remaining coconut milk.

8. Form small bowls with the banana leaves. (Alternately, you can put the leaves themselves into small ceramic bowls or ramekins).

9. Gently pour the fish stew into the banana leaf bowls.

10. Add the duck egg/coconut mixture on top of the *amok*. Steam the *amok* for 10 mintues in the banana leaves.

11. Top with chilies and green onions, and for a touch of extravagance, add salmon roe.

Kaw Sach Chrouk (Braised Pork Belly)

Kaw Sach Chrouk   Photo: Chef T

This dish, *kaw sach chrouk* (braised pork belly) has flourished across Southeast Asia. Individual countries and communities prepare it differently, but the foundation is pork: belly, shoulder, shank, butt, etc., depending upon what is available and within a family's means.

This is a humble dish, but the love for it transcends socioeconomic class. Everyone loves *kaw sach chrouk*. When my mom would cook it, the delicious aroma would wake everyone in the house up! When it finally came time to eat, we would gather around and go for seconds and thirds until the rice pots were empty and our stomachs full.

My version has a lighter broth but otherwise is true to my mom's recipe. Here is my caramelized, braised pork belly for all to enjoy.

Chef T's
Kaw Sach Chrouk (Braised Pork Belly)

Cook time

35 min prep time
1 hr. cooking time

Serves: a lot of people

(Or a few people who go
back for seconds and thirds)

INGREDIENTS

2 whole garlic bulbs
4 shallot bulbs

5 cups water
½ cup *skar thnout*
  or brown sugar
¼ cup oyster sauce
½ cup soy sauce
¼ cup dark sweet soy sauce

2 pounds pork belly
6 large duck eggs

1 ½ pound bamboo shoots
½ pound baby corn
6 whole star anise
1 pinch coriander
1 ½ tbsp freshly ground black
  mric Kampot (Kampot pepper)
Salt to taste

Cooking directions:

1. Add peeled and chopped garlic and shallots to a large pan.

2. Add the water and sugar. Simmer.

3. Add oyster sauce, salt, pepper, soy sauce, dark sweet soy sauce, and fish sauce. Heat until the mixture starts to caramelize, but make sure the sugar doesn't burn.

4. Hard boil the duck eggs and set aside.

5. Add the pork belly to the sauce, stirring continuously while the meat cooks. Add more pepper as you stir.

6. Add the bamboo shoots and baby corn.

7. Peel the duck eggs and add them whole to the stew.

8. Add the star anise and coriander. Simmer for about 30-40 minutes.

Delicious with ជ្រក់បន្លែ (*chrouk banlae* - pickled vegetables)!

Chapter 4: Sweet ផ្អែម

Nom Plae Ai
(Sticky Rice Dumplings with Palm Sugar)

Nom plae ai is what I would call a "dessert amongst desserts." That is, it is a delicacy not served on a regular basis. Rather, Cambodians make *nom plae ai* when there is a special occasion: a holiday gathering or a festival for example. It is Dr. Su's favorite, however, so I had to include it in this book!

When someone makes *nom plae ai*, the whole house becomes fragrant with the wonderful aroma of these sweet rice balls. And, one bite and the soft glutinous rice gives way to a burst of melted *skar thnout* inside.

My mother would make *nom plae ai*, but only occasionally. Not only is *nom plae ai* reserved for special occasions, it also tricky and time-consuming to make correctly. I remember helping her, waiting impatiently for it to be finished so I could experience the delicious taste of toasted coconut and palm sugar.

In this recipe, I put my own flare on it and modernized it, but I am also a fan of it in its most basic preparation.

Nom plae ai

Photo:
Sovanna Mao

19

Chef T's
Nom Plae Ai

PREP TIME: 1 hr 20 min
COOK TIME: 45 min

SERVES 6-8

INGREDIENTS

(for the dough)	(for the filling)	(for garnish)
4 cups sweet (glutinous) rice flour 1 ½ cups hot water	6 oz. *skar thnout* (palm sugar) 6 tbsp coconut oil 6 tbsp room temp water	½ cup toasted coconut shavings Toasted sesame seeds

Cooking directions:

Part I:

1. Place the *skar thnout* (palm sugar) into a pan, and then add water.

2. Heat on medium heat, slowly stirring until the sugar has dissolved.

   Add coconut oil and mix. Remove from heat and let the mixture stand for a few minutes until it thickens.

3. Once it is cool enough for you to touch, but not cold (once cold it will begin to harden), form the sugar into small (approx. ¼ inch) balls.

4. Place sugar balls on aluminum foil or wax paper and set aside.

Part II:

1. Pour rice flour into a large bowl. Slowly pour in the hot water, stirring slowly and continuously until a gelatinous dough forms.

2. Gently knead the dough for about 5 minutes. Cover with plastic wrap and set aside.

3. Take a small piece of dough and flatten it out with the palm of your hands to form a small, flat circle.

4. Place one of the palm sugar balls in the middle of the circle. Gently roll the dough so that it covers the palm sugar, taking care not to tear it.

5. Repeat until all palm sugar filling is used. (If you have extra dough, you can roll it without filling it, or you can save it for other desserts!)

6. In a large pot, bring water to a boil. Once boiling, slowly drop in the sugar-filled rice flour balls. While they are cooking, prepare an ice bath in a separate bowl. When the balls float to the top, they are finished.

7. Scoop finished balls into the ice bath, then remove and roll them in the coconut shavings and/or toasted sesame seeds.

I like to sprinkle a little powdered sugar on the balls to give the dessert a delightful, extra sugary bite.

Chapter 5: Inspirations ការបំផុសគំនិត

I am inspired by everything around me: people, places, events, sounds, smells, textures. I absorb everything and this is reflected in my cooking, my art.

For example, I have a deep understanding of Asian culinary flavors and techniques, yet I am very inspired and influenced by French and Italian cultures and cuisines as well. And of course, I add a touch of Americana to my dishes. Many of my creations could be described as "fusion," since I draw from my love for many types of foods and life experiences. I could write an entire book about my inspirations, but here I will focus on just a few.

Family

As I mentioned, my mother, Pheakdey Anna Mean, did the majority of the cooking in my house as I was growing up. I owe a lot of my knowledge of Khmer flavor profiles and techniques to her. I also need to give respect to my grandmother, Kim Ly Mean. I treasure my memories with her, many of which revolve around cooking. Watching both of them instilled in me my love of cooking from the time I was a toddler. When I was about four, I was *daam baay* (cooking) myself, making eggs and searing steak, especially when my mom and grandmother were out of the house. I'm lucky I didn't burn the house down!

From these two strong women, I started to learn about the different Khmer tastes: that is, there are spices and flavor combinations that are uniquely Khmer, and you really have to learn them from someone who knows how to create and use them. ដោយសេចក្ដីគោរពដ៏ខ្ពង់ខ្ពស់បំផុត ខ្ញុំសូមអរគុណ។ Thank you, *Mak* and *Yiey*.

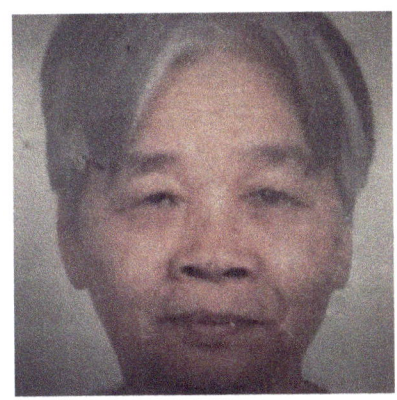

Left: My mother,
Pheakdey Anna Mean
Right: My grandmother,
Kim Ly Mean

Photos courtesy of Chef T

While my father only cooked once in a while (see section on *somlor machu kroeung sach koh*), he inspired me in a different way. It was my father, Savon Kon Ouk, who taught me how to read and write in Khmer, even as I was growing up in the United States. I am grateful to him for giving me that cultural grounding. Language is so important in understanding the nuances of culture, so I am fortunate that he made sure I knew that part of my Khmer heritage. ដោយសេចក្ដីគោរពដ៏ខ្ពង់ខ្ពស់បំផុត ខ្ញុំសូមអរគុណ។ Thank you, *Pa*.

My parents and grandmother have had an enormous influence on me and my cooking. Because of them, I knew that no matter where I lived or where I went in life, I wanted to include Cambodia and Khmer culture in my work.

I now have a family of my own: my beautiful wife, Baky, and my son, Phoenix. I named my son Phoenix because I love the mythology of the phoenix rising from the ashes. I hit a really low point in my life: you could even say I hit rock bottom, but now, I truly feel like I have been reborn – I am a Rising Phoenix. My wife and son inspire me every single day. I live not only for myself, but for them.

My logo:
The Rising Phoenix

Image courtesy of Chef T

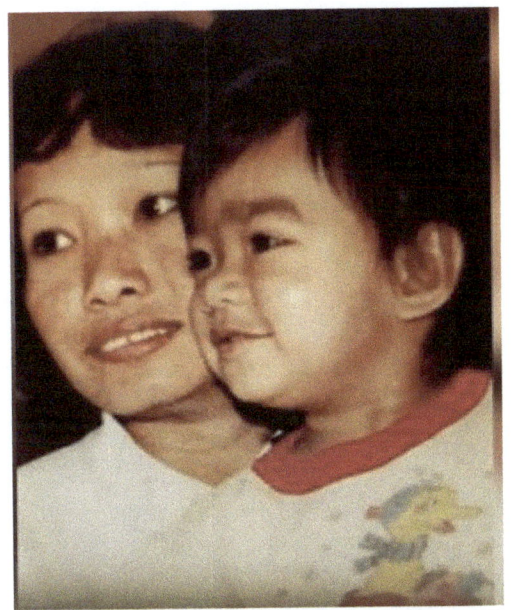

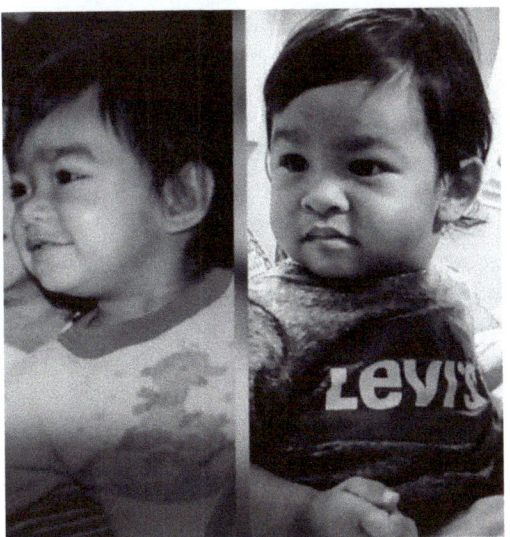

Clockwise from top left:

1. My wife, Baky with my newborn son, Phoenix Tarak.
2. My mother holding me at age 2.
3. Me at age 2 juxtaposed next to my son at age 2.
4. My beautiful family.

Photos on pages 23 – 26 courtesy of Visoth Tarak Ouk ("Chef T") and Baky Sar

My Family

ក្រុមគ្រួសាររបស់ខ្ញុំ

Food and Family
by Baky Sar

I was born in Manila, Philippines, while my family was at a transitional camp on our journey to be resettled in the United States. My parents survived the Khmer Rouge regime, and their memories of that time affect them still today. When I was 6 months old, my parents and siblings and I relocated to Long Beach. I am one of seven children.

It wasn't easy growing up in east Long Beach, but I knew the value of hard work and I pushed myself to achieve my goals. I am a licensed cosmetologist and began my career in West Hollywood. I have been able to work with several celebrities and my art has even been published.

Like Chef, I grew up in a home where food is the love language. I was so lucky to be able to have authentic Cambodian food, with recipes passed down from my grandmother to my mother. I love anything with *kroeung*, as well as *prahok ktis* and other special Khmer dishes: *amok*, *somlor kari* with carrots and potatoes, *somlor kakou*. I am so fortunate to be able to eat these foods, cooked by mom. Her cooking is so authentic and delicious.

Interestingly, I first met Chef when he invited me to a Sinn Sisamouth-themed dinner gathering just before Khmer New Year one year.[3] We had mutual friends but had never crossed paths. We became fast friends but didn't begin a relationship right away. Well, Chef was determined to build a relationship other than friendship; I, on the other hand, initially had no interest because I was focused on work and building my brand. But I was soon drawn in by his passion, generosity, and kindness.

Family is very important to both of us, especially now that we have started our own family. Our son, Phoenix, is the love of our lives. I thought I knew what true love was until I first held my son. It was in that moment I swore I would always protect him and do my best to give him everything. He's growing up so fast!

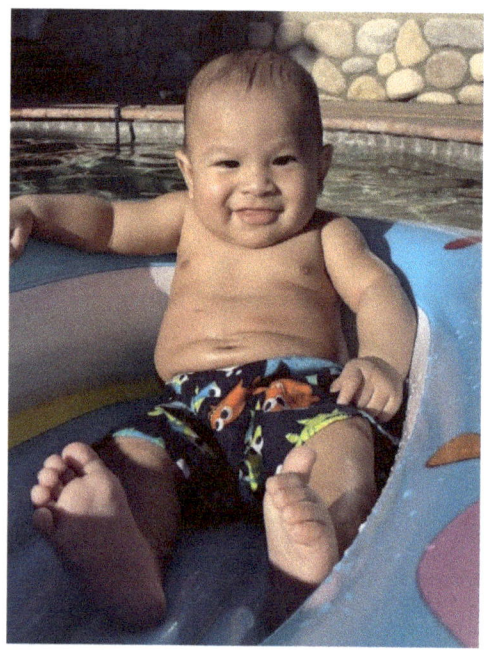

Above: Phoenix, @ age 7 months
Above right: Phoenix, @ age 2 ½ yrs.
Right: Phoenix, @ 3rd birthday party

Chef T and I are both artists in our own right and have many things in common, including a love of food!

We are so blessed to both be working doing something we each love, and to have our beautiful son.

Our lives haven't always been easy, but we have each other.

Community
By Chef T

I was born Visoth Vebolgotharak Tarak Ouk in Chonburi camp in Thailand. Chonburi was the "holding" camp for refugees who had been cleared for resettlement, whether to the United States, Canada, Australia, or elsewhere. From Chonburi, my family (my grandmother, my mother and father, my aunt and uncle, my older sister and myself) relocated to Oakland, California. But when I was eight, we (now a much larger family with the addition of more siblings) moved to Long Beach, which became and remains my home.

Long Beach is one of the most diverse cities in the country, and while far from perfect, there are things that bind me to it; one of those things is that Long Beach is home to Cambodia Town. "Cambodia Town" refers to a 1.2-mile stretch in Long Beach along Anaheim Street, between Atlantic and Junipero Avenues. While 1.2 miles may seem small in the scheme of things, for Cambodians in the U.S., it is huge. In Cambodia Town, Khmer writing appears on signs hanging above shop doors, from markets to donut shops to auto repair garages. Restaurants serve Khmer food, and those in the know can request special Khmer dishes not on the menu. Fruits and vegetables that are "exotic" to most Americans but common to Cambodians can be purchased there. People walking down the street speak not only English and Spanish, but also, Khmer language. Furthermore, Cambodia Town refers to a much larger psychological and conceptual space in which places and people are recognizable, familiar; a space that embraces an historically- and emotionally-connected community.

In July 2011, community members and local officials gathered at the intersection of Atlantic Avenue and Anaheim Street to unveil a sign reading "Cambodia Town," reaffirming not only the presence but also the significance of Cambodians in Long Beach. This was especially meaningful because while Long Beach has the largest number of Cambodians outside of Cambodia itself, the overall population counts are small compared to other ethnic groups in the city, such as LatinX or African Americans. Yet "smaller" does not mean "minor," because Cambodians are an integral part of the fabric of Long Beach.

I have always said that I wanted to help put Cambodian food "on the map;" and now, there actually is a map of places to try Cambodian food in Long Beach! And what is so exciting is that it was created by Cambodian youth, who have begun to recognize their Cambodian identity as a point of pride, not prejudice. I get emotional thinking about that – having faced racism, discrimination, and shame for most of my youth. The youth identified key business and artistic spaces in the community, including social and cultural organizations as well as restaurants and shops. They designed the map, entitled "The Spirit Within," and produced it for distribution themselves. I am awestruck by their professionalism and creativity.

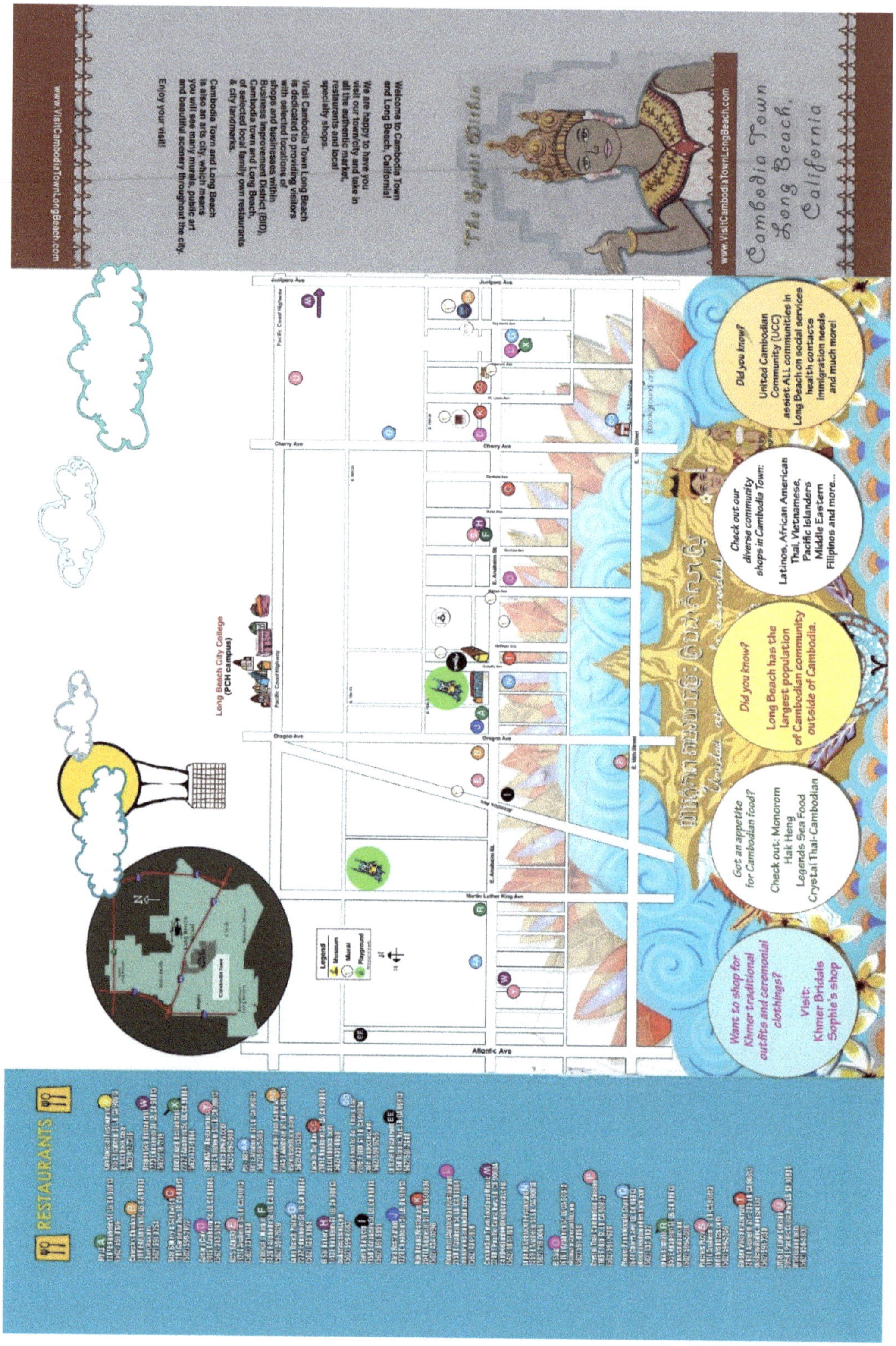

"The Spirit Within." Map of Cambodia Town (front side),
created by Cambodia Town Youth.
Map © 2018 by Visit Cambodia Town Long Beach. For a larger version of the map, go
to http://www.visitcambodiatownlongbeach.com/map-2/
Reproduced with permission.

Chapter 6: Table Talk with Chef T

To bring this book to a close, we wanted to allow readers to hear our own voices. To that end, we share with you both some of the questions about the process of putting the book together and reflections about the future of Cambodian cooking in the U.S., asked by Dr. Su and answered by Chef T.

Dr. Su: Chef T, what was the process of writing this book like for you? Did you revisit many of your childhood memories while you were thinking about what recipes to include? Take us through what was going on in your mind and heart.

Chef T: I couldn't have been as articulate in narrating the stories for this book without your help, Dr. Su! While thinking about which recipes I wanted to highlight and then in writing them down, a flood of feelings came over me. I always tell people that food connects you to your past, but I didn't truly experience that for myself until we started this project. In writing things down, I clearly remembered the smells and aroma associated with specific dishes, and how I felt when I ate them. Food connects us to our memories, and memories to our hearts. Thinking about my past and going through my old papers with hand-written recipes on them that I've been collecting for more than 20 years was a wonderful yet emotional rollercoaster. My recipe book is as thick as a bible! And it holds just as many stories: love stories, sad stories, happy stories – all kinds of memories live in there. As I turned each of the pages to select my favorites, I felt like I was re-living my childhood and young adulthood. It was like getting into a food-coma time machine!

Dr. Su: Chef T, what do you see as the future of Cambodian American cooking? Do you believe Cambodian food will become more well known? What challenges do you see in making this happen? What would be your greatest hope or dream?

Chef T: With Cambodian food, we have to open ourselves up to new cooking methods and food evolution. I believe that it is very important to be authentic and true to the original recipes, but also important to evolve as times move forward. Cambodian restaurant owners need to tackle new ideas, new methods to improve their menus--and also, to advertise themselves. Even within the diverse landscape of Long Beach, Cambodian eateries lag behind other ethnic restaurants. We seem somewhat stuck in an old-style format of running a restaurant, with few using technologies and techniques to manage sales, and little training in terms of server and table etiquette. There is nothing wrong with the way it's being done, but to attract a wider audience, we have to meet a broad range of customer expectations.

Also, I think it's essential that respect for the food industry is instilled in us at home. Families should recognize that the food industry is just as (and maybe even more so) necessary as other industries. To be called "Chef" is a prestigious and honorable title, not a low-ranking or shameful title. Parents need to be proud of their kids wanting to become chefs. In my case, I didn't feel like my profession was seen as very impressive, and there were many who rather than encouraging me, discouraged me. But Cambodian food is amazing, and we need more great Cambodian chefs to share it and take it to new heights. I hope that I have started to put Cambodian food on the map, especially in Cambodia Town.

Dr. Su: Chef T, your son, Phoenix, is growing up so quickly! He is about the age now that you were when you started showing an interest in cooking. Has your son shown any signs of wanting to follow in your footsteps? And, does he like Khmer food?

Chef T: I can't believe that my son is almost 4. Wow! At 4 I knew I wanted to cook, and really did know basic cooking techniques already. My son definitely does not like Khmer food at the moment, although I will surely change his taste profile as soon as he grows up a bit!

But in general, when I am cooking, I see him get very interested in what I'm doing. He gets very excited with all his food toys and utensils and cutlery, and pretends to slice and dice and present things to my wife and me. He loves watching kids cooking with their parents in videos on his iPad.

I don't know if he wants to become a chef, and I certainly won't push him, but I will definitely show him how to cook a couple of Cambodian dishes, to teach him about his heritage. It's really important to me to teach him about Khmer culture, including food, but also the Khmer language, spoken and written, like my father did with me. I want him to be fluent in speaking, reading, and writing Khmer. I am fluent; so shall he be. I want him to have that cultural grounding—even in my darkest moments, I never forgot that I am Cambodian, I am Khmer. I won't ever let him forget who he is, or where he came from. He is my pride and joy, my son.

Dr. Su: Chef T, your story is so inspirational. What advice do you have for our youth, especially but not exclusively Khmer youth, as they try to navigate what often seems a very harsh and uncaring world? What would you like them to take away after reading this book?

Chef T: The advice I have for our youth is probably something they've already heard, but maybe they haven't really internalized it, really felt it. My advice is that you need to follow your dreams. I spent so many years navigating the streets, protecting a code, a street code.
I put aside my passion for cooking, even though it was burning within me. I was trying to fight it and got caught up in negative energies and living an alternate life, and didn't follow the path I knew was right for me.

In the end, following my passion and my dream of becoming a chef was the one thing that truly made me happy. All the things I thought were important didn't fulfill me. My advice, to youth, older men and women, anyone: find something that you love, that gives you purpose. The path that you will carve out for yourself and the resulting journey that you will take will be momentous. It may be challenging, and sometimes you may want to give up, but the ending--fulfilling your dreams--will make the struggles worthwhile. If I had only 24 hours to live, I would cook. Of course, I would want to be with my family, but I would also create (my art is cooking) until the sun sets on my life. After reading this book, I hope people realize that everyone has the power inside them to achieve their biggest dreams. Rise up and meet your destiny. Nothing is impossible. If a street gang member can become an Executive Chef, nothing in this world is too far out of reach.

NOTES and CREDITS

NOTES

[1] In the U.S., our people are known as Cambodians. In-country and amongst ourselves, we use the native language term "Khmer" (pronounced "khmae"). In this book, we use both.

[2] Timeline information compiled from various sources: *Cambodian Tribunal Monitor*; BBC News Asia; U.S. Dept. of State; Documentation Center of Cambodia; National Institute of Statistics, Royal Government of Cambodia.

[3] *Sinn Sisamouth* was an influential and highly prolific Cambodian singer/songwriter from the 1950s to the 1970s, widely considered the "King of Cambodian Music." Sinn Sisamouth, along with Ros Serey Sothea, Pen Ron, Mao Sareth, and other Khmer artists, was part of a thriving pop music scene in Phnom Penh that combined elements of Khmer traditional music with contemporary global sounds. Diasporic Cambodians of all ages continue to listen to his music today.

PHOTO AND IMAGE CREDITS*

Cover photos: Maly Uch and Sokunthea Oum
Dedication page: photo courtesy of the Ouk family

p. vi:	Southeast Asia Map image by muchmania/Adobe Stock
	Cambodia map by Christine Su/SEARCH
p. 4:	Cambodian foods and condiments, photo by Mary Kheng
p. 5:	*Kroeung* ingredients, photo by Sokunthea Oum
p. 7:	*Prahok*, photo by Pakse/Adobe Stock
	Trey riel (aka Siamese Mud Carp) photo by BigYoi/Wikimedia
	Skar thnout, photo by Sovanna Mao
p. 8:	*Ampil*, photo by YarikL/Adobe Stock
	map with Kampot province highlighted, image by NordNordWest/Wikimedia
	Black, white, and red peppercorns, photo by TravelPhotography/Adobe Stock
p. 10:	Young Visoth with his father in Oakland, photo courtesy of Chef T
p. 12:	*Somlor machu kroeung sach koh*, photo by Maly Uch
	Trakuon in bowl, photo by Christine Su
	Uncooked *trakuon*, photo by Maly Uch
p. 13:	*Somlor machu yuon 'royale,'* Photo by Chef T
p. 15:	*Amok* in banana leaf cups, photo by Maly Uch
	Amok "king," photo by Chef T
p. 17:	*Kaw sach chrouk*, Photo by Chef T
p. 19:	*Nom plae ai*, photo by Sovanna Mao
pp. 21-26:	All photos and images courtesy of Visoth Tarak Ouk ("Chef T") and Baky Sar
p. 28:	"The Spirit Within." Map of Cambodia Town (front side), created by Cambodia Town Youth. © 2018 by Visit Cambodia Town Long Beach. Reproduced with permission.

*All appropriate permissions and licenses for the photos and images in this book have been obtained.

CONNECT WITH
THE CHEF AND THE WRITER

If you would like to know more about Khmer food, Chef T's recipes, Cambodia Town or the Cambodian community in Long Beach, the Khmer Generations Project, future publications, book launches, speaking engagements, and more, please go to https://www.khmergenerations.org/contact-kgp or scan the QR code below and provide us with your contact information.

Thank you so much for your love and support.

Chef T's Instagram: @therisingphoenixlbc562
Chef T's Facebook: https://www.facebook.com/visothtarakouk

33